Romancing the WEST

The Life of the American Cowboy
in Photographs and Verse

Photography by Robert Dawson

Text and Editing by Rose Caslar

As a young boy growing up in Texas I would often spend my summer afternoons lying on my back in a nearby open field starring up at the clouds as they drifted by. I would daydream of riding across the west with my friends in search of big adventures like my heroes Hopalong Cassidy and Roy Rogers. As I have grown older I have realized that I have spent most of my life chasing those daydreams and trying to capture those adventures the best way I knew how and that was through the lens of my camera.

I would like to take this time to thank my heroes and they include Hopalong and Roy, my wife Julie, my stepdaughter Jessica and all the people that have helped me in this and my previous books in preserving those moments in time. In looking back on this road that we have traveled I see now that we were all, in our own way, Romancing The West.

Robert Dawson

Published by RD Publishing, Inc.
P.O.B. 477
Joseph, OR 97846
(541) 263-1413
Website: dawsonphotography.com
Email: dawsonphoto@eaglecap.net

Photography - Robert Dawson
Text & Editing - Rose Caslar

Design & Production - Bryan Daws
D2 Design Communication Studio

Printed in Hong Kong

ISBN 13 # : 978-0-9678881-3-2
ISBN 10 # : 0-9678881-3-1

Robert Dawson Photography
P.O.B. 477
Joseph, OR 97846
541-263-1413

FORWARD TO ROMANCING THE WEST

I have been a fan of Robert Dawson since we met almost a decade ago. His eye for creativity surpasses all the photographers that I have worked with in my years of advertising and sponsorship.

Dawson doesn't just take a photo he creates an image that stimulates your emotions and expands your imagination. His use of light and composition reminds me a lot of the great western artist Charlie Russell. If there is such a term as Photo Artist, Dawson fits the profile to a "T".

His dedication to the western Heritage and attention to detail ensures the authenticity of his photographs. I often look forward to meeting with Dawson just to see his latest portfolio and I catch myself savoring the moments in time that his talent has captured through the lens of his camera.

So my advise to you is to sit back in your easy chair and let Robert Dawson take you on a ride through the life of the American Cowboy.

Al Dunning

Let yourself linger over Robert Dawson's enchanting photographs and you will be drawn into the heart of the Golden West. In this book, hooves drum, lariats sing, sunsets blaze, and dust settles silently to the ground. Cowboys are glimpsed both impassioned and in repose, but whether he is thundering up a rocky gully or drinking in a spectacular view, each is perfectly at ease among his animal companions, as elemental as the forces that shape his native canyons, peaks, and plains.

Dawson's idyllic images invoke the adventurous spirit that has made the cowboy a folk hero and Western icon, but he also invites his viewers to enter the cowboy dream themselves. At times, he catches an intimate nearness to his untamed subject, almost allowing viewers to feel the smooth warmth of a horse's coat or dull thud of hooves beneath them.

To enhance the romantic tones of Dawson's pictures and enlighten readers on some nuances of daily cowboy life, complementary songs, poems, and excerpts were selected. Many of the songs were penned when the Wild West was still unfenced; some are so old as to be of unknown authorship and have earned the earmark "traditional." These are songs that cowboys have always sung and will continue to sing. The lyrics and music survive because their themes of longing, loss, and love of tough horses have never stopped resonating with those who share the cowboy heart. In addition, several modern buckaroos lend their voices in rhyme as a reminder that some folks still persist in this horseback occupation.

The stunning beauty and enticing freedom of cowboy life is not altogether a thing of the past, as can be seen through Dawson's camera. He has ridden along the cowboy trail to bring back some of the glorious solitude, quiet romance, and high adventure of the Golden West. Enjoy.

Rose Caslar, *Editor*

COWBOY LEXICON

Beef – *A steer older than four years.*

Bunch-quitter – *An independent horse or cow who does not abide by the herd instinct and will leave a gathered herd.*

Cavvy – *A ranch's herd of saddle horses, available for use by all that brand's cowboys.*

Chokin' the biscuit – *To grab onto the horn when a horse bucks, also known as "pullin' leather."*

Chuck – *Food, grub, chow.*

Cold-backed – *A horse who bucks briefly after being saddled. Usually, after a short "warm-up," a cold-backed horse will settle into being ridden.*

Dogie – *Motherless calf.*

Hunker – *To hide or shelter oneself; applicable to man or stock.*

Jig-trot – *A long striding trot riders take up when they need to cover a large area in a day. Notably used by cowboys in Nevada, where the pasture sections are generous.*

Pace – *An a-typical gait in which the horse moves his feet in parallel pairs, as opposed to the normal diagonal pairs, at the trot. Some uncatchable wild horses in cowboy lore were pacers, such as the Pacing White Stallion, known for his speed and legendary endurance.*

Ringy – *Used to describe the panicky, sometimes aggressive state of a wild horse or cow confined to a corral.*

Romal – *A braided rawhide whip or "popper," attached to the end of a set of rawhide or leather reins. Up to five feet long, it was used as a quirt on horses, or even to reach out and slap a slow-moving cow.*

Scratch – *To spur a horse*

Sulled up – *Used to describe a horse or cow that refuses to move. Derived from the word 'sullen.'*

Swell-fork – *Used to describe the front part of the saddle that the horn sets upon. A swell-fork saddle flares wide below the horn, whereas a "slick-forked saddle" is narrow.*

He was the worst bronco I've seen on the range,
He could turn on a nickel and leave you some change.
While he was buckin' he squealed like a shoat,
I tell you, that outlaw, he sure got my goat…

I lost my stirrup, I lost my hat,
I was pullin' leather as blind as a bat;
With a phenomenal jump he made a high dive
And set me a-winding up there in the sky.

I turned forty flips and came down to earth
And set there a-cussin' the day of his birth.
I know there's some ponies that I cannot ride,
Some of them living, they haven't all died.

From "Strawberry Roan," Curley Fletcher 1914

O BURY ME NOT ON THE LONE PRAIRIE

"O bury me not, on the lone prairie,"
these words came sad and mournfully
From the pallid lips of a youth who lay on his dying bed,
at the close of day.
"It matters not, so I've been told, where the body lies,
when the heart grows cold,
So friends please grant this wish to me:
O bury me not on the lone prairie."

"O bury me not on the lone prairie,
where the coyotes howl and the wind blows free;
In a narrow grave, six by three,
O bury me not on the lone prairie.

"O bury me not" – his voice failed there,
but we took no heed of his dyin' prayer;
In a narrow grave, six by three,
we buried him there, on the lone prairie.

Traditional

LOVE

In a hoss they call it loco
In a man they call it love –
Spillin' milk while readin' mash notes
Written by a turtle dove.
He talks about her night and morning
Raves about her to the cow
Til' the critter kicks the bucket,
Well, you just can't blame her, can you now?
He used to be a top hand cowpoke,
Straight and girl-shy to a fault,
Till old cupid got him hog-tied,
And now he just ain't worth his salt.
What loco does to hosses
Is what love's sweet poison does to men,
And it takes a sudden shock like marriage
Till they find their wits again!

Unknown

A ranch horse must be strong enough to carry a man all day over all kinds of rough country. A typical cowboy isn't all that heavy, but he wears chaps and rides a twenty-five pound saddle that might have a slicker, canteen, and lariat tied onto it. A tired, stumbling horse could mean injury, death, or lost cattle to a cowboy riding through rocks, varmint holes, or darkness. The old time, big cattle outfits had a regular cavvy or remuda, so riders changed horses at noon. If he had night duty, he changed again at night. The same horse was never ridden for two days in a row, so each rider had at least four horses in his string and possibly six or seven.

11

To supply a ranch, whereon a stock of ten thousand cattle are kept, with the necessary saddle horses, a stock of at least one hundred and fifty broodmares should be kept. The geldings are only used for the saddle...Their food is grass exclusively, and many of them are as utterly unfamiliar with the use of grain as they are of Latin, and will often, when kept in the north, starve to death before they will eat grain. Almost every one has to be taught to eat corn or oats by placing a quantity in a small muzzle-shaped sack and fastening it over the animal's nose...

Joseph G. McCoy, Historic Sketches of the Cattle Trade, 1874.

The cowboy needs a set of hooves to ride across the range,
But the bright-eyed colt he's chosen disputes being trained.

The start is tough on both sides, a rough test of two wills -
Who'll be settin' higher when the dust finally stills?

Man has proved his self to be the most stubborn critter of all,
He's ready for the colt's wild temper, his flyin' buck and bawl.

But there's a secret to horse breakin' beyond just bein' tough,
This buster's got to know when the colt has had enough.

Maybe after buckin', boltin' and puttin' on quite an act,
The colt gets pretty tired and tries a more cooperative tact.

Right then, our cowboy knows to do just the same –
He hangs the quirt back on the horn, eases up on the reins.

His kicks and pulls get gentler, and the colt, he listens,
A little trust is building, and understanding quickens.

This bronco's learned that workin' together is an easier game
And there's plenty of work to be done for two partners on the range.

Rose Caslar

A CANYON HORSE

When you're starin' down your chapleg
Half a mile or so,
And wishing he weren't slick shod
Nor his feet balled up with snow,
And you're diggin' through your pockets for your makin's or a chew,
He'd steady as a pile of rock.

But then, he's catty, too,
When you're comin' through the bad place
Or you're riding off the top.
He keeps his feet a-moving 'cause there ain't no place to stop.

And when the wreck's progressing
Or the chase is in full swing,
When your lead mule and a switchback
Are fighting for your string;
He's got a brain beneath them ears,
And if you've got one, too,
You'll just keep your seat and loose your feet
And then come riding through.

Down south in swell-fork country,
Where they jig-trot half the day,
And they ride a string of horses down,
But just go out to play,
They make them ponies ante
And they brag 'em to the sky;
But I wouldn't trade 'em
If the sky was twice as high.

Andy Fairchild

A Cowboy's Life

A cowboy's life is a very dreary life,
Some say that it's free from all care,
Rounding up the cattle from the morning 'til the night,
In the middle of the prairie so bare.

The wolves and the owls with their terrifying howls,
Disturb us in our midnight dream,
While we're lying on our slickers on a cold and rainy night,
Way over on the Pecos stream.

I used to roam around, but now I stay at home,
Cowpuncher's take my advice;
Sell your saddle and your bridle
Quit your roving and your travel
And marry you a pretty little wife.

Traditional, Texas

Thunderin' hoofs across the range,
Sunburned hides and faces,
Twisters spinnin' east and west,
And cowboys runnin' races.
"Scratch your broncs, you ridin' fools,"
A big whoopee they give'er,
"We're wild and woolly, full of fleas,
And bound for Powder River!"

From "Powder River, Let'er Buck," Powder River Jack Lee

THE NIGHT HERDING SONG

Oh slow up, you dogies, quit your roamin' around,
You've wandered and trampled all over the ground
Go graze along, dogies, and feel kinda slow
And don't be forever on the go.
Move slow, dogies, move slow.

Oh say, little dogies, when you goin' to lay down,
Quit this forever siftin' around?
My limbs are weary, my seat is sore,
Oh lay down, dogies, like you've laid down before.
Lay down, dogies, lay down.

Traditional, Texas

She dashed madly down through the gulch one day, standing erect upon the back of her unsaddled cayuse, and the animal running at the top of its speed, leaping sluices and other obstructions – still the daredevil retained her position as if glued to the animal's back, her hair flowing wildly back from beneath her slouch hat, her eyes dancing occasionally with excitement…

Now she dashed away through the gulch, catching with the light long breaths of the perfume of flowers which met her nostrils at every onward leap of her horse, piercing the gloom of the night with her dark lovely eyes, searchingly, lest she should be surprised; lighting a cigar at full motion – dashing on, on, this strange girl of the Hills went, on her flying steed.

E.L. Wheeler, Deadwood Dick on Deck; or,
Calamity Jane, the Heroine of Whoop-Up, 1885.

He left the young man these few words;
his last cowboy refrain:

He said, "Don't you look back, son, if it causes any pain.
Don't dwell on the hard times, your soul don't need the rain.
Always ride with a warmth inside that'll calm a stormy day;
Never let that love for life ever slip away…

From "Don't Look Back," C.D. Nichols

LIFE IN THE SADDLE

Coyotes howlin' somewhere off in the distance,
Coyotes howl, a breeze is singin' softly with an old hoot owl.
In the early mornin' twilight, he gently snugs that cinch tight,
Prepared to face the dawnin' of another day.
He's a foot in the stirrup and mounts the bay.

Set him high, slide into that saddle and set him high.
He's got a cold-backed jump or two, you better get him by.
And then after a quick storm, no one comes to no harm,
He'll line right out on the trail of the old divide.
Aint' a thing he'd rather do today than ride.

Life in the saddle, he never will retire,
A horse and a healer, the only company he requires.
From the back of his horse he'll see it through,
Cause he's proud of his life of a buckaroo.

C.D. Nichols

RED RIVER VALLEY

From this valley they say you are going,
I shall miss your bright eyes and sweet smile;
For they say you are taking the sunshine
That has brightened my path for a while.

Come and sit by my side if you love me,
Do not hasten to bid me adieu,
Just remember the Red River Valley
And the cowboy who loved you so true.

There never could be such a longing
In the heart of a poor cowboy's breast,
As dwells in this heart you are breaking
While I wait in my home in the West.

Traditional, Canada

HOME ON THE RANGE

Oh give me a home, where the buffalo roam
And the deer and the antelope play
Where seldom is heard a discouraging word
And the skies are not cloudy all day.

Where the air is so pure, the zephyrs so free;
The breezes so balmy and light,
That I would not exchange my home on the range
For all of the cities so bright.

How often at night when the heavens are bright
With the light from the glittering stars
Have I stood here amazed, and asked as I gazed
If their glory exceeds that of ours.

Brewster Higby, 1873

WHOOPEE-TI-YI-AYE GIT ALONG LITTLE DOGIES

As I was out walking one morning for pleasure,
I spied a young cowboy a-ridin' along.
His hat was pushed back and his spurs were a-jinglin'
And as he approached he was singing this song.

Whoop-ee-ti-yi-aye, get along little doggies,
It's your misfortune and none of my own.
Whoop-ee-ti-yi-aye get along little doggies,
You know Wyoming will be your new home…

If I ever marry it'll be to a widow
With fourteen children, not one of my own;
If I ever marry it'll be to a widow
With a great big ranch and a ten-story home.

Traditional

PRETTY PAULINE

Come all ye young cowboys come hear my sad tale,
Never leave your true love to ride the big trail.
Stay away from the big trail, my friend it don't pay;
If you've got a sweetheart you can lose her that way
Pretty Pauline, I dream of her yet.
Out on the big trail I try to forget,
But the love that we shared is still hauntin' me;
Pretty Pauline, will I never be free

I kissed her goodbye at the old garden gate;
As I stepped on my pony she told me she'd wait.
But little did I know as I loped away,
That she'd find another the very next day

I'm still on the big trail a doin' my share,
A pushin' the herd to the railroad up there,
But the mem'ry hangs on wherever I roam
Of my pretty Pauline that sweetheart back home

Remember this warnin' I give you my friends:
Stay off of the big trail you can lose in the end;
You can lose your true love just the way I lost mine,
When you ride to far places and leave your true love behind.

Walt LaRue

COWPOKE

I'm lonesome but happy, rich but I'm broke,
And the Lord knows the reason I'm just a cowpoke.

From Cheyenne to Douglas, all the range I know,
'Cause I drift with the wind, no one cares where I go.

Well, I ain't got a dime in the these old worn out jeans,
So I'll quit eatin' steak and go back to beans.

But I'll win me a ten-spot in Prescott I know,
Just a spurrin' a bronc in the big rodeo.

Some evenin' in springtime, a filly I'll find,
And I might spend all summer with her on my mind.
But I'll never be branded and never be broke,
I'm a carefree, range-ridin', wild-driftin' cowpoke.

Traditional

I am roving cowboy, I've worked upon the trail
I've shot the shaggy buffalo and heard the coyote's wail.
I have slept upon my saddle, all covered by the moon;
I expect to keep it up, dear friends, until I meet my doom.

From Western Pioneer," Traditional